T0149494

Revelation
A Twelve-Week Study

Julie P. Fitchuk

WESTBOW
PRESS®
A DIVISION OF THOMAS NELSON
& ZONDERVAN

Cover photo by Todd Pulliam @Pulliam Photography.
Used by permission.
Harvest time in my beloved southern Indiana.
The intersection of Highways 3 and 356.

Scripture quotations are taken from the Holy Bible, New International Version®, NIV®. Copyright © 1973, 1978, 1984, 2011 by Biblica, Inc.™ Used by permission of Zondervan. All rights reserved worldwide.

Author's photograph by Evelin Herbstreit.

WestBow Press books may be ordered through booksellers or by contacting:

WestBow Press
A Division of Thomas Nelson & Zondervan
1663 Liberty Drive
Bloomington, IN 47403
www.westbowpress.com
1 (866) 928-1240

ISBN: 978-1-5127-6964-7 (sc)
ISBN: 978-1-5127-6966-1 (hc)
ISBN: 978-1-5127-6965-4 (e)

Library of Congress Control Number: 2016921299

Print information available on the last page.

WestBow Press rev. date: 10/08/2019

Dedication

This book is lovingly dedicated to my sweet lady friends who attended the first small groups I led on the Book of Revelation. Your friendship has meant so much to me and I will never forget your enthusiasm. My heart was thrilled as I watched your eyes sparkle every time we studied together. May our wonderful God and Father continue to bless your lives, and your beautiful families.

Thank You

To my wonderful Lord and Savior
Thank you for coming.
Your constant care and mercy will forever be my strength.
My heart is filled with gratitude.

To my parents, Toi and Richard
Thank you for being true followers of Jesus Christ.
Never compromising, never wavering and
always filled with love and compassion.
Your example leads the way for future generations.

To my friend, Tom Haley III
Thank you for your helpful advice and insight regarding this study.
Your valuable time and talent are very much appreciated.
May God bless you immensely.

Contents

Prologue

My husband reminded me the other day that I was talking about the Book of Revelation early in our marriage. I had forgotten that. We were in our early 20's. I am much older now and in the last few years, the Lord has renewed my love for the book.

One day while praying about what to share with our congregation during worship time, I began reading Revelation 5. My heart began to race, and the pure joy I felt was indescribable. I had read this book many times, but this time was different. It was like the words leapt off the page, entered my heart and started a fire.

So, on that Sunday morning, I decided to read all of Chapter 5 to the congregation, before singing any songs. The band and singers expected me to end the reading and then play through the chorus of our first song. However, by the end of Chapter 5, I was so excited about the scripture, that I just started singing the first song. I sang with no band playing, no singers singing and I had started the song in the wrong key.

This twelve-week study in no way will answer every question you may have. It is meant only to be a starting point for you, and to hopefully whet your appetite to want to study the Book of Revelation more. It is formatted so that you may study as a group or by yourself. Music is always fun and meaningful when added.

As knowledge increases (Daniel 12:4) and time keeps advancing, we learn more and more about this prophetic book. I intend fully to always keep an open mind regarding the events of this book, and you should too. Why, you ask? Because I don't know it all. It will be good for you as you study, to look at every angle, even angles you may not agree with. Scholars, theologians, you and I may not all agree and reach the same conclusion. But one thing our beliefs must do, is line up with scripture.

The Holy Spirit is the one who helps us understand the Word of God. So please pray before you study each time. Ask the Holy Spirit to help you think clearly and not get distracted. Remember to keep Jesus at the center of the book. He is after all, the Alpha and Omega and everything in between.

When you're finished I sincerely hope that you will have learned more than your heart could have imagined. I know when you're finished; you will see your Savior in a glorious new way.

Jesus is worthy-the only one worthy of praise! He is
the only one worthy to open the scroll in Revelation 5.
All worship belongs to him, all glory and honor.

Blessed is the one who reads aloud the words of this prophecy, and blessed are those who hear it and take to heart what is written in it, because the time is near.

Revelation 1:3

Introduction

Week 1

Note: Day 1–If you are doing this study as a group, please read aloud to the class, this introduction and also pages pertaining to Revelation 1 Week 1. Then read Revelation 1 aloud to the class and answer the Revelation 1 questions together.

The word *revelation* simply means to unveil or reveal. This is exactly what the Book of Revelation does. It reveals Jesus to us. He is our focus. Our main goal during these next twelve weeks is to get to know Him better. The Book of Revelation is a beautiful picture of our wonderful Savior, his glory, his majesty and his judgment. First and foremost, he loves. That's why he was born as a baby and why he died on a cross. He loves people-all people.

Scripture says that we are all sinners, in need of a Savior.

> For all have sinned and fall short of the glory of God. (Romans 3:23)

> But God demonstrates his own love for us in this: While we were still sinners, Christ died for us. (Romans 5:8)

For God so loved the world that he gave his one and only Son, that whoever believes in him shall not perish but have eternal life. For God did not send his Son into the world to condemn the world, but to save the world through him. Whoever believes in him is not condemned but whoever does not believe stands condemned already because they have not believed in the name of God's one and only Son. (John 3:16–18)

When you receive Jesus as your Savior, you receive the "seal" of his salvation, which is the third person of the Holy Trinity, the Holy Spirit. (We will talk about this more, later in the study.) It is the Holy Spirit who helps us to understand everything God is speaking to us. If you have never done so, please prayerfully consider asking Jesus to be your Savior, and ask the Holy Spirit to help you understand this important book of the Bible.

Here is a prayer you can pray when you want to receive Jesus:

Dear Jesus, I understand that I am a sinner and in need of a Savior. I am sorry for my past mistakes and I ask you to forgive me. I put my faith in you and ask you to be the Lord of my life. Help me to live for you and to fulfill the destiny you have for me. In Jesus' name, Amen

Welcome to the family of God! Welcome Home!

Revelation 1

Week 1

Through the inspiration of the Holy Spirit, the apostle John wrote this wondrous book. There are other theories that suggest another person named John wrote the book, but most scholars believe it is the apostle. In Revelation 1:1, 4, and 9, and also in 22:8, the author identifies himself.

Most interpreters think the time of this writing was AD 95. Roman officials were beginning to enforce the worship of their emperor, Caesar. Because John would not be silent about Jesus, he was banished to the island of Patmos. As Christians were holding onto their belief that Christ − not Caesar − was and is Lord, they were beginning to face persecution themselves.

There are four major interpretations:

Preterists (meaning past or beyond) say the end-time prophecies in the book were fulfilled by AD 70. They teach that Christ's second coming has already taken place, as have the Tribulation and the final judgment. There is also a tendency to believe that "the church" has replaced Israel in God's plan.

A historical view on the Book of Revelation claims that the book describes things taking place as far back as Patmos, and ending with the end of the world. This view means interpreting symbols and figures as metaphors for people, places and events. For example, East and West Germany are "the wound that had been healed" in Revelation 13:3.

Futurists take the stance that these events take place in the end times, and for the most part are taken literally. For example, the false prophet *is* the false prophet.

An idealist or allegorical position takes the view that the book is symbolic and, merely a fight between good and evil.

In this study, we will follow the perspective of the futurists. We will find a few symbols in the book, but you will come to understand what they are. One reason John wrote using symbols very well could have been so Roman officials would not recognize that he was speaking of them. Another may be because God wants us to study his Word. The use of symbols really makes a person search out correct answers and right teaching. Searching the scripture draws you closer to Jesus.

For this study we will also take the view that Christ followers (Christians) are taken to be with Christ before the Tribulation begins. This is known as *Pre-Trib*, a rapture or gathering together of Christ followers before the Tribulation.

Some people believe in *Mid-Trib*, a gathering together of Christ followers in the middle of the Tribulation. Others believe in *Post-Trib*, a gathering after the Tribulation.

Let me explain why I believe in Pre-Trib.

The seven-year period known as the Tribulation will be the wrath of God poured out. The "earth dwellers" will be subject to God's judgment. True Christ followers are not appointed to wrath.

Please Read 1 Thessalonians 1:10,
5:1–11, and Romans 5:8–11.
Also Read Matthew 24:36–38 and Luke 17:26–28.

According to the scripture in Matthew and Luke, people are eating, drinking, marrying and being given in marriage. In the Book of Luke, they are also buying and selling and planting and building. As we study Revelation you will see just how bad life becomes on the earth. I don't believe people will be having fun and holding festive parties during the Tribulation; therefore I think the rapture will occur before the Tribulation.

If you believe in the rapture of the church before the Tribulation, you may have been taught that it takes place at Revelation 4:1("Come up here") because the church is not mentioned after Chapter 3:22 (except at Rev. 22:16 when Jesus says who the testimony is for). And after Revelation 4:1, the people of the earth are called "earth dwellers" or "inhabitants."

Whether we agree on Pre-Trib, Mid-Trib or Post-Trib is not so important in our study. What is important, however, is that we agree to keep Jesus at the center.

Please Read Revelation 1 Aloud!
Answer Revelation 1 questions together if studying as a group.

Revelation 1
Week 1 (Day 1)
Please answer these questions together in class.

1. What can we learn about John?
    Matthew 4:21–22_____
    Matthew 17:1–3_____
    John 19:25–27_____
    Acts 4:13_____

2. The revelation is from whom?

3. What does it mean to testify to something?

4. Who is testifying?

5. What does the promise in verse 3 mean to you?

6. What do you think "take to heart" means in verse 3?

7. According to verse 5, Jesus has freed us from _____ by his _____.

8. Give your opinion as to why the people in verse 7 are "mourning."

9. Who are "those who pierced him?" (Read Matthew 26:1–5 and Romans 3:23.)

    (For further reading on "those who pierced him," see Zechariah 12:10–14.)

10. Who does John say he is in verse 9?

11. Why is he on the island of Patmos?

12. Describe what John saw among the golden lampstands in verses 10–16.

13. Who is speaking to John in verses 17 and 18, and what is being said?

14. Who are the seven stars in verse 20?

15. What do the seven lampstands represent?

Revelation 2 and 3

Week 2

In the last lesson, you read about the rapture of the church. The church is comprised of people who follow Jesus Christ and who call him Savior and Lord.

Please Read 1 Corinthians 12:27–28 and Ephesians 1:22–23.

The word *raptus* is a Latin word meaning to seize. It is found in the Latin Bible. The Greek word for raptus is *harpazo,* which means to seize, claim for one's self eagerly or to snatch out.[1] Most scholars believe that the New Testament was written in Greek with the exception of Matthew, possibly written in Aramaic.

In 1 Thessalonians 4:13–18 we read about "being caught up together." This is how theologians conclude that there is a rapture or a seizing of the church.

Last week you read why I conclude there will be a rapture before the Tribulation. However, if I am wrong, along with millions of other

---

[1] Thayer and Smith. "Greek Lexicon entry for Harpazo." "The KJV New Testament Greek Lexicon." www.biblestudytools.com

people, you must remember to hang on, hold on, and remain faithful to Jesus until your death!

In Chapters 2 and 3 we are introduced to seven churches. Jesus tells John to write what he sees, and then "send it" to the churches. You will notice each letter begins with, "To the angel of the church." There are different ideas as to whom these letters are actually written. Some people think these angels are actually angels. Others believe these letters are addressed to the pastors of the churches.

Angel in Greek is aggelos (pronounced ang'elos). *Strong's Exhaustive Concordance Of The Bible* says: "a *messenger*; especially an *"angel"*; by implication a *pastor*: angel, messenger."[2]

Whether these are supernatural beings or the pastors of these churches, remember that Jesus is the one who holds the seven stars, and He is the one who guides these churches.

And although the Lord was speaking to the angels of these churches, he was also speaking to individuals. "Whoever has ears, let them hear."

So you can see, at the outset of our study, people have different views. Don't get discouraged by this. It just means people are studying the scripture and attempting to be accurate. That is a good thing! The angels of these churches may be a subject you study further on your own, to decide exactly what your belief on this is.

---

[2] James Strong, Strong's Exhaustive Concordance Of The Bible. (Hendrickson Publishers, Inc. 2007), 1599

While you read through these seven letters addressed to the seven churches, please examine your heart, and apply these instructions to your own life. The Lord tells the people of these churches to "repent" several times. Repentance is an act of the heart.

Let's take a look at true repentance for a moment.

Please Read Joel 2:12–14.

Although Joel is writing to the people of Judah, calling them to repentance, this can certainly be a message from the Lord to modern-day people as well.

In this scripture, The Lord is saying to return to him with all of your heart. In verse 13, he says, "Rend your heart and not your garments."

In biblical times when people were in mourning, sometimes they would "rend their garments." Rend means "to remove by violence" and "tear forcibly apart." According to the *Merriam Webster Dictionary*.[3] We know we can't rip our hearts from our chests and tear them into pieces. Our only response can be to dissect or judge it while it still beats within us. If you've accepted Jesus as your Savior and committed your life to him, that would be step number one.

Warren Wiersbe in *The Wiersbe Bible Commentary* describes repentance so beautifully;

---

[3] Merriam-Webster Dictionary. (Merriam-Webster, Inc. 1994), 620

He writes, "We must correctly distinguish regret, remorse and true repentance. Regret is an act of the mind; whenever we remember what we've done, we ask ourselves, "Why did I do that?" Remorse includes both heart and mind and we feel disgust and pain but we don't change our ways. But true repentance includes the mind, the heart and the will. We change our mind about our sins and agree with what God says about them; we abhor ourselves because of what we have done; and we deliberately turn from our sin and turn to the Lord for his mercy."[4]

> Create in me a pure heart, O God and
> renew a steadfast spirit within me.
> Psalm 51:10

What needs to be removed from your heart? Are you angry with someone you need to forgive? Do you need to ask someone to forgive you? Are your motives and friendships pure? Are you addicted to something that you should not be? Are you bitter, scornful or negative? Are you a worrier or a gossip? Are you prideful?

Spend a few moments in prayer with your Heavenly Father. Allow the Spirit of Almighty God to help you "Rend your heart."

> My sacrifice, O God, is a broken spirit;
> a broken and contrite heart you, God, will not despise.
> Psalm 51:17

---

[4] Warren Wiersbe, The Wiersbe Bible Commentary: Old Testament. (Published by David Cook 2007), 1324

Day 1

Now we begin our study of the seven churches, with many questions to answer. You will be given some background for each church. Then you can read the scripture for the day and answer the questions. You may want to study one church a day for the next seven days, so you don't get behind in the twelve-week study. All of these churches were located in Asia Minor, present day Turkey.

The ancient city of Ephesus is located near modern-day Selcuk. This church was pure in its doctrine. They were very hard workers and diligent at keeping false teachers out of the church. Jesus commends them for not tolerating the Nicolaitans. The Nicolaitans were thought to be a group of people within the church who taught that spiritual freedom allowed them to practice idolatry and immorality. The teachings were believed to be similar to the teachings of Balaam (which you will learn more about at Pergamum on Day 3). Further, it is believed that this group got its name because they followed a man named Nicolas. Nicolas was from Antioch, and a convert to Judaism. He is mentioned in Acts 6:5. It is possible that Nicolas was one of the first seven deacons in the church at Jerusalem, but the evidence is circumstantial.[5]

This church is not tolerating false teaching, but they have lost their first love for Jesus.

---

[5] The NIV Study Bible. (Zondervan Grand Rapids, Michigan 2011), 2151

In 2 Corinthians 11:2 and Ephesians 5:25–27, we read that the church is thought of as the bride of Christ. If you think of Revelation 2:1–7 in this context, as a marriage, you can begin to understand how important it is to always remember the "love you had at first." Sometimes marriage may become somewhat stale, and may be somewhat boring. But if you remember the love you had at first for your spouse and "do the things you did at first," it makes a world of difference.

Read Revelation 2:1–7

1. How does Jesus describe himself in verse 1?

2. What does Jesus know about the church in Ephesus?

3. Please read the following scripture and write down what you learn about perseverance.
   Romans 5:1–5, Romans 12:12, Galatians 6:9, Colossians 1:11–13, James 1:12.

4. How does scripture say we test spirits, false teachers and false prophets?
   (Read Matthew 7:15–20, Acts 17:10–12, 2 Timothy 2:15, 1 John 4:1–6 and 2 John 7–11.)

5. What did Jesus hold against the church in Ephesus?

6. What three things did Jesus say for them to do in verse 5?

7. What did Jesus say he would do in verse 5, and what do you think that means? (Read Matthew 5:14–16.)

8. What will the victorious receive? (Read Genesis 2:9 and 3:22.)

Day 2

Smyrna is now known as modern-day Izmir. The name Smyrna is said to have come from the word *myrrh*. The word *myrrh* comes from the Arabic word *murr,* which means bitter. What I've read about myrrh is that to make it, the harvester must wound the tree over and over again. Myrrh is considered precious oil. It was given to our King as a gift in Matthew 2:11. Myrrh is made by crushing the ingredients. T.D. Jakes has said, "When pressure is applied, you find out what you're made of." The church in Smyrna was learning this because they were being crushed by persecution. One reason their members were being persecuted could well have been because they refused to call Caesar lord. If they refused to call Caesar lord, then it is possible they would not have been permitted to be employed. This would have caused them to live in poverty, which Jesus said he knew about in verse 9. However, Jesus calls them rich.

Keep in mind as you study Smyrna- Jesus knew what they were going through (as he does with every church). But he actually tells this church what the Devil is about to do. So, Jesus is aware of what is ahead for them. All the while, he is in complete control! Jesus opens this letter by saying, "These are the words of him who is the First and the Last." At the end of the letter to the church at Smyrna, he says he will give the faithful, "life as your victor's crown." Smyrna was a city who participated in the annual athletic games, so they could identify with being first, being last and receiving the victor's crown.

Many scholars believe the second death spoken of in verse 11, means after the Tribulation and after the thousand-year reign of Christ. People will stand before the throne of God to be judged. This is known as the great white throne judgment of Revelation 20:11–15. The people who have never repented or trusted Jesus Christ as Savior are thrown into the lake of fire.

<u>Read Revelation 2:8–11</u>

1. Who are these the words of?

2. What does he know about the church in Smyrna?

3. As a believer in Jesus, how can you be in poverty and rich at the same time? (Read 2 Corinthians 6:4–10 and 8:9.)

4. What is the "synagogue of Satan"? (Read Romans 2:17–29.)

5. Read the following verses on suffering. Write down what they mean to you.
    Please add any others that are meaningful for you.
    Job 36:15, Psalm 34:18, Psalm 147:3, John 15:18, 2 Corinthians 1:3–11.

6. In verse 10, what does Jesus tell them is about to happen?

7. What are his instructions to this church?

8. What do the faithful and victorious receive?

Day 3

Pergamum, is now known as the city of Bergama. Pergamum had the first temple dedicated to Caesar, and promoted cult worship. The city had at least four temples dedicated to the worship of false gods. One was to Zeus, one to Athena and one to the healing god, Aesculapius, whose emblem was an entwined serpent on a staff. This is still the symbol for the medical profession today. When Jesus said, "where Satan has his throne," in verse 13, he could have been referring to these temples built for false gods.

This church was strong in its faith even though its members lived among cults. Jesus, however, is aware that the church has allowed some compromising people to infiltrate it. While the church at Ephesus was diligent in keeping compromising teachers out, the church in Pergamum was not. In reading about the church in Pergamum, you will see that Antipas, a faithful witness of Jesus, was martyred in that city. Tradition holds that Antipas was roasted to death in a bronze kettle.

It is interesting to note that the victorious in these passages receive "hidden manna" and also a "white stone." Hidden manna contrasts with the food used for idol worship. White stones in ancient times were used by judges to vote acquittal for a person on trial. White stones were also used like a ticket to gain admission to a feast.

Read Revelation 2:12–17

1. In the opening of the letter to Pergamum, what does Jesus have?

2. Verse 13 says, "I know where you live." Does this comfort you or scare you and why?

3. What was Balaam's advice (teaching) in Numbers 31:15–16?

4. How many died due to this compromising doctrine? (Read Numbers 25.)

5. Some of the people were still holding to the teaching of the _____?

6. What was this church told to do in verse 16?

7. What did Jesus say he would do if they didn't? (Hebrews 4:12–13.)

8. What do the victorious receive? (Matthew 4:4 and John 6:32–33.)

Day 4

Thyatira is modern-day Akhisar. This was the hometown of Lydia, "dealer of purple" spoken of in Acts 16:14. Thyatira had a temple dedicated to Apollo, the sun god. Notice at the opening of the letter to this church, Jesus says, "These are the words of the Son of God."

At this church there is a false prophet whom Jesus calls Jezebel. The church is permitting her to mislead the believers. Since the Jezebel from the Old Testament had long since died, this is someone who is teaching what Jezebel taught. The teaching was thought to be once again, along the lines of Balaam. Jesus calls it "Satan's so called deep secrets." (We learned about this teaching back at Pergamum.)

Read Revelation 2:18–29

1.   How does Jesus present himself in the opening of this letter?

2.   What are your thoughts regarding what he says about himself?

3.   What does Jesus say he knows about this church?

4.   Who was the woman named Jezebel in the Old Testament? (Read 1 Kings 16:29–31, 2 Kings 9:22 and 9:30–37.)

5.   Who else is suffering because of her sin?

6. What does Jesus tell them to do in verse 22?

7. What does Jesus tell the "rest" to do in verses 24–25? (Read Isaiah 41:13, 1 Thessalonians 5:21–22 and Hebrews 10:23–25.)

8. What do the victorious receive?

Day 5

Sardis is modern-day Sart. In biblical times it was the capital for the kingdom of Lydia. The kingdom of Lydia covered about a third of the western part of Asia Minor (modern-day Turkey). Sardis was 1500 feet above the lower valley. Because of its location, it was considered safe from its enemies. Since it was considered a secure area, the watchmen for the city would sleep at their posts. Their enemies were then able to invade them. The church at Sardis is also sleeping, which is why Jesus tells them to, "Wake up!" It has a reputation for being alive, but it is dead. It seems that it had grown complacent. It was content with the way things were, and did not see the need for change. The Lord was also telling this church to "strengthen what remains" before it dies altogether.

The "seven Spirits of God" spoken of in Chapter 3:1(also found in Rev.1:4 and 4:5) could be a reference to Isaiah 11:2.

Please Read Isaiah 11:1–2.

The "shoot" and the "Branch" here are actually referring to Jesus. Isaiah lists some of the attributes the "shoot" and the "Branch" will have. 1. "The Spirit of the LORD will rest on him." 2. "The Spirit of wisdom and" 3. "of understanding," 4. "the Spirit of counsel and" 5. "of might," 6. " the Spirit of knowledge and" 7. " fear of the LORD—"

Whether a reference to Isaiah or not, these scriptures still speak to the fullness and completeness found in God *and* in the number seven. The number seven is God's number for perfection. The victorious in Sardis receive garments of white. Sardis was known for making woolen products. So Jesus speaking about garments, in verse 4, would have resonated with the people. If you are a true Christ follower, your name will never be erased from the Book of Life. Revelation 3:5 is assurance of that, and you can rest assured that Jesus Christ knows his own children.

Read Revelation 3:1–6

1. What do we learn about Jesus in verse 1?

2. Again, who are these stars that Jesus holds? (Revelation 1:20.)

3. The church in Sardis had a reputation for _____
   but were _____?

4. What five things does Jesus tell them to do in verses 2–3?

5. If the church in Sardis does not wake up, what will Jesus do?

6. What is the significance of wearing white garments?
   (Read Romans 13:11–14, Jude 23 and Revelation 19:7–8.)

7. The victorious will be like whom?

8. What does Jesus say he will do for the victorious?

Day 6

Philadelphia, modern Alasehir. The meaning of course is "love of the brethren" or "brotherly love." This church has little strength, yet it is remaining true and not denying the name of Jesus. The Lord encourages this church by saying He is the one who opens and shuts doors. This may mean doors of opportunity for ministry and for employment. It may also mean the door to the Kingdom of God. After all, He is the one who opens hearts and minds. Like the church in Smyrna, the church in Philadelphia also had to deal with people whom Jesus called the "synagogue of Satan." These people claimed to be Jews, but they were not. This church was located in an earthquake-prone area, so when Jesus says "The one who is victorious I will make a pillar in the temple of my God," they knew that meant security and stability, along with a firm foundation as spiritual pillars in the faith.

Read Revelation 3:7–13

1. How does Jesus introduce himself in verse 7?

2. Why do you think holding the key of David is meaningful?(Read Psalm 89:3–4, Isaiah 9:6–7, Micah 5:2, Luke 1:32 and John 7:42.)

3. For you, personally, what does it mean that the one "who is holy and true," opens and shuts doors?

4. Jesus opened the door to what in Acts 14:27 and 1 Corinthians 16:9?

5. Why will the church at Philadelphia be kept from the hour of trial that is coming to the whole world?

6. Why is the hour of trial coming?

7. Jesus will make the victorious what, in verse 12?

8. Read Galatians 2:9. Who are the people in this verse, known as "pillars"?

Day 7

Laodicea is near modern Denizli. Laodicea was a very wealthy city, known for its banks, medical school and famous for an eye salve and textile industry. Located to the north of Laodicea was the city of Hierapolis, which was known for its hot springs. To the south was the city of Colossae, known for its pure cold water. Laodicea did not have an adequate way to obtain water. As water traveled to Laodicea from the hot springs in Hierapolis, it became lukewarm. As cold water from Colossae traveled to Laodicea, it also became lukewarm, which is why the people of Laodicea would have understood the importance of being either hot or cold.

The church in Smyrna thought itself poor, but Jesus said they were rich. This church thinks its people are rich because they are in need of nothing, yet Jesus tells them that they are poor. When Jesus counsels this church "to buy from me gold refined in the fire," could he be suggesting this church needs some persecution? In some cases a little hardship or persecution will turn a heart toward God. My father likes to say, "Hardship builds character."

Read Revelation 3:14–22

1. These are the words of whom and what does this mean to you?

2. Why is Jesus about to spit these people out of his mouth?

3. Feeling a bit "lukewarm" in your faith? Read 2 Timothy 1:6. What does Paul tell Timothy to do?

4. Jesus called this church wretched, pitiful, poor, blind and naked. Why?

5. What did he tell them to do about it?

6. What do we learn about suffering and persecution by reading Romans 5:3–4 and 1 Peter 1:6–7?

7. Who does Jesus rebuke in verse 19?

8. Why is it good for Jesus to rebuke and discipline? (Read Job 5:17, Psalm 94:12, Proverbs 3:11–12 and Hebrews 12:5–11.)

9. Jesus is standing where, and what is he doing in verse 20?

10. What do these victors receive?

In summary and regarding all the churches:

1. What churches did Jesus say good things about?

2. What churches were rebuked?

3. Which churches does he say he loves?

We've reached the end of our study on the churches. I pray you have learned a significant amount about these seven churches, and that you have taken to heart the important instructions given to each.

If you are doing this study as a group, discuss your answers and then,
Please Read Revelation 2 and 3 Aloud!

Revelation 4 and 5

Week 3

Last week you read from the Book of Joel, where God says to "Rend your heart and not your garments." Surgery on the heart means to cut out bad motives, removing anything that might not be pleasing to God. With true repentance, you change your mind about sin, and turn away from it.

This week in Revelation 4 and 5 we see how worship is done around the throne of God. Praising God and worshiping him never ends in Heaven. So, we had better get comfortable doing it.

Every church I have ever been to has set time aside during the service to sing to the Lord. Some churches call this time, "Praise and Worship." Many churches sing with a full band accompanying them, while others may use just a guitar, piano or even sing songs a cappella. Singing and playing instruments is a wonderful way for us to minister to the heart of the Father, and it can be good practice for the real thing one day. As we take our final breath here on earth and enter that beautiful city, the only thing we will have to offer the King of Glory, will be our worship.

We know that God appreciates music because he himself is a singer. Zephaniah 3:17 says that God rejoices over his people with singing. Think of it! The creator of the universe sings!

"Praise" music is often thought of as upbeat, having a faster tempo and adds a little excitement to the atmosphere. When you praise someone, you are expressing appreciation, showing respect and approval. "Worship" music is thought to be just that, worshipful. It is slower in tempo, a little more quiet, and often brings the heart to deeply reflective moments.

> God is spirit, and his worshipers must
> worship in the Spirit and in truth.
> John 4:24

If we are going to worship God in the Spirit and in truth like this scripture tells us, we must understand our own heart. God already knows what is inside our heart. He knows our thoughts before we think them.

Please Read Psalm 139.

For me, always checking my motives for why I am doing something helps me in my every day worship of God. Worshiping him is much sweeter when your motives and your heart are pure before him. In her book, *Extravagant Worship*, Darlene Zschech writes, "I understand true worship to be when one's spirit adores and connects with the

Spirit of God, when the very core of one's being is found *loving* Him, lost *in Him*."[6]

Consider what true worship means to you. When others around you are raising their hands in praise to the Lord at church or another religious function, what is your heart telling you to do? When others are kneeling or dancing? Be truthful with yourself. Do you want to raise your hands, kneel or dance, but don't? Then you are not worshiping truthfully. You must be true to who God has made you to be, as you worship him. If it means sitting still, then do that. Hebrews 13:15 says to "continually offer to God a sacrifice of praise." Could your sacrifice be kneeling when you don't want to, or possibly raising your hands when not feeling comfortable doing it? As I studied the Book of Revelation so intently over the last year, I have found myself face down on the floor in worship. He is the Almighty God, the Maker of Heaven and Earth. Sometimes I just have to get as low as I can, to show Him the honor and adoration He alone deserves.

Take a deep breath. That breath is from God. In Genesis 2 we read that God breathed into the nostrils of man, and he became a living being. God alone is why we are breathing right now. He truly does deserve all praise. When you look back over your life-yes, even the painful, messy, sinful events; you will come to understand the love and power of our Majestic King Jesus. He washes and cleanses where there was once only sin and infection. He rebuilds and restores. He teaches and guides. He alone can make all things new. He fills the empty places in our hearts and in our lives. He mends the broken

---

[6] Darlene Zschech, EXTRAVAGANT WORSHIP (BETHANY HOUSE 2001, 2002), 27

heart and makes straight the path of the sinner. If that is not enough, He raises the dead to life again! He died for us! He rose for us!

Worshiping in spirit and in truth is a position of the heart. No matter how you do it, it is what we are told to do in scripture.

Ways to Worship our God and King

Psalm 29:1-2 Ascribe to the LORD, you heavenly beings, ascribe to
the LORD glory and strength.
Ascribe to the LORD the glory due his name; worship
the LORD in the splendor of his holiness.

Psalm 46:10 Be still, and know that I am God

Psalm 47:1 Clap your hands, all you nations; shout to God with cries
of joy.

Psalm 47:6 Sing praises to God, sing praises; sing praises to our King,
sing praises.

Psalm 66:1 Shout for joy to God, all the earth! Sing the glory of his
name; make his praise glorious!

Psalm 95:6 Come, let us bow down in worship, let us kneel before
the LORD our Maker

Psalm 134:2 Lift up your hands in the sanctuary and praise the
LORD.

Psalm 149:3 Let them praise his name with dancing and make music
to him with timbrel and harp.

Read Revelation 4

1. The one sitting on the throne had the appearance of what? (Read Ezekiel 1:26–28.)

2. What was surrounding the throne?

3. Who do you think the twenty-four elders could be?

4. Please list the twelve sons of Jacob found in Genesis 49.

5. What is the name of the son not included in an inheritance and why? (Read Deuteronomy 18:1–2.)

6. Please list Jacob's two Grandsons in Genesis 48:1–6.

7. How many disciples were there? (Read Matthew 10:1–4.)

Disclaimer: I cannot say for certain that the elders are the twenty-four you have just listed; however it is a fun thing to note.

8. The elders had crowns of gold on their heads. For what reasons are crowns given?
    (Read 1 Corinthians 9:24−27, 2 Timothy 4:7−8, James 1:12, 1 Peter 5:1−4 and Revelation 2:10.)

9. What was coming from the throne and what do you think this says about God?

10. Please compare the creatures from Revelation 4:7−9 with the creatures found in Ezekiel 1:10−11.

11. What does giving glory, honor and thanks to God mean to you and how are you doing this in your own life?

12. What do the elders do when the creatures give glory, honor and thanks to him who sits on the throne?

Read Revelation 5

1. Please describe what was in the right hand of the one on the throne?

2. What do you think is the importance of writing on both sides and being sealed with seven seals?

3. What did John do when he realized no one was worthy to open the scroll?

4. What is the significance of "the Lion of the tribe of Judah" and the "Root of David" being mentioned in verse 5? (Read Genesis 49:8–9, Isaiah 11:1–3 and 11:10, also Matthew 1:2–6.)

5. Who was the Lamb in verse 6? (Read John 1:29, 36, 1 Corinthians 5:7 and 1 Peter 1:19.)

6. Describe the Lamb.

7. What did the elders and creatures do after the Lamb took the scroll?

8. Each one had a _____ and they were holding golden bowls of incense that are _____.

9. In verse 12, what is the Lamb worthy to receive?

10. What "new" song can you write and sing to the Lamb? Please try and express your deepest gratitude and admiration.

After discussing the answers,
Please Read Revelation 4 and 5 Aloud!

Revelation 6 and 7

Week 4

As you begin the study for this week, please pray for the lost and the backslidden. Ask our beautiful Savior to open the eyes of the blind and the hearts of the misled. There are millions of unsaved people who need what we as Christ followers have. They need Jesus Christ.

Last week we learned about praise and worship. We learned how important it is to give both to the Lord. We learned about the different ways to do that. We can worship God by clapping our hands, dancing, singing, bowing, kneeling or by just being still. As believers in Jesus we know he is worthy to receive all of these things. And although he is merciful, kind and so loving, in the chapters ahead we will meet him as the righteous judge. He has been patient long enough, and now it is time to bring the "earth dwellers" under submission. If they do not repent, they will be lost forever. Jesus said,

> Do not let your hearts be troubled. You believe in God, believe
> also in me. My Father's house has many rooms; if that were
> not so, would I have told you that I am going there to prepare
> a place for you? And if I go and prepare a place for you, I will

come back and take you to be with me that you also may be where I am. You know the way to the place where I am going.

John 14:1–4

The Holy Bible is filled with stories of people who were saved out of very difficult circumstances. Noah and his family were saved from the flood. Lot and his family were saved when Sodom and Gomorrah were destroyed. Rahab and her family were spared. There is safety in God. We do not need to be afraid. We need to be in prayer for lost souls.

Many theologians believe that when a seven-year peace covenant with Israel is confirmed, the Tribulation will begin.

He will confirm a covenant with many for one 'seven.' In the middle of the 'seven' he will put an end to sacrifice and offering. And at the temple he will set up an abomination that causes desolation, until the end that is decreed is poured out on him.

Daniel 9:27

From this passage we learn that the antichrist (He) confirms a covenant, and Israel is promised peace for seven years. Scholars believe this means seven actual years. This confirming of a covenant will not only reveal who the antichrist is, it will begin the opening of the seven seal judgments. From this verse we also learn that Jews are sacrificing and bringing offerings to their temple. We can also see from this verse that halfway through the seven, the antichrist puts an end to their sacrifices. Then he goes into the temple and declares himself to be God; this is what is known as the "abomination that causes desolation."

Please Read Matthew 24:15 and 2 Thessalonians 2:4.

<u>Read Revelation 6</u>

1. When the <u>first seal</u> was opened by the Lamb, what happened?

2. What was the rider on the white horse given and what is he carrying?

3. Who do you think this rider is and why? (Read Daniel 11:36, Matthew 24:4−5, 23−25 and 2 Thessalonians 2:1-12.)

4. What does Jesus have on his head in Revelation 19:12 and what is his weapon of choice in Revelation 19:15?

5. When the <u>second seal</u> was opened by the Lamb, what happened?

6. What was the color of the second horse, and what was its rider given?

7. When the Lamb opened the <u>third seal</u> what happened?

8. What was this rider holding and what was being said?

9. When the Lamb opened the <u>fourth seal,</u> what happened?

10. What power were Death and Hades given?

(For more reading on horses see Zechariah 1:7–11 and Zechariah 6:1–8.)

11. When the <u>fifth seal</u> was opened what did John see?

12. What happened to these people and why?

13. What were they told to do?

14. There was a great earthquake when the <u>sixth seal</u> was opened. What happened in the sky and on the earth?

15. Who was hiding, where and why?

Right before the seventh seal is opened in Chapter 8, scholars believe John takes what is known as a parenthetical pause. This pause takes place during all of Chapter 7 when the seal judgments are briefly interrupted. John sees other important things taking place. These are things that the reader needs to know and be aware of.

In Chapter 7, we read about angels who hold the winds, and about the 144,000 people who are God's servants. We also meet a group of people so large no one can count their number. The close of Chapter 7 brings us to the close of the parenthetical pause and with Chapter 8, judgment begins taking place again. Remember our God is an equal opportunity God, and gives everyone a free will to choose him or not to choose him.

<u>Read Revelation 7</u>

1. What are the four angels doing in verse 1?

2. Verse 2; what power had been given to these angels?

3. What is the significance of having the seal of God?(Read 2 Corinthians 1:21–22 and Ephesians 1:13–14.)

4. Compare 2 Corinthians 1:21–22 and Ephesians 1:13–14 with Ezekiel 9:1–6. Write down what you learn.

5. Write down where the 144,000 come from in Revelation 7:4?

6. Please read Revelation 14:1–5, and write down what you learn about the 144,000.

7. Genesis 49, names the twelve sons of Jacob. Please list them again here.

8. As you review the list of Jacob's twelve sons you've listed for question #7, and his grandsons listed in Genesis 48:1–6, whose names are omitted in the Rev. 7:5–8 list?

(For more reading on these Tribes see Exodus 23, Joshua 16 and Judges 1. To read more on the Tribe of Dan see Judges 18.)

9. The "great multitude" in verse 9, came from where? (Also see verses 13–14.)

10. What did the angels, elders and four creatures do in verse 11?

11. Will the worship of God and the Lamb in this chapter affect the way you worship? How and why?

12. Please write what verses 15–17 mean to you personally.

After discussing your answers,
Please Read Revelation 6 and 7 Aloud!

Revelation 8 and 9

Week 5

As Chapter 8 begins, we read that when the seventh seal is opened, there is silence in Heaven. This silence is very unusual. Up to this point music, singing, worship and praise have been nonstop. There have been creatures that constantly say:

> Holy, holy, holy
> is the Lord God Almighty,
> who was, and is, and is to come.
> Revelation 4:8

Some people believe that during this silence is where the rapture occurs. They believe this is the Mid-Trib point. Others believe the middle of the Tribulation starts at Chapters 10 and 11.

You will notice in Chapters 8 and 9 as the trumpet judgments begin, in some instances, God allows only a third of things to be affected. As with the seal judgments, God is being patient with the "inhabitants of the earth." For some, there is still time to repent.

Please take a moment to pray for anyone you know who needs Jesus. Pray for our nation and all nations of the earth. Pray for the leaders of every nation.

When I shut up the heavens so that there is no rain, or command locusts to devour the land or send a plague among my people, if my people, who are called by my name, will humble themselves and pray and seek my face and turn from their wicked ways, then I will hear from heaven, and I will forgive their sin and will heal their land. Now my eyes will be open and my ears attentive to the prayers offered in this place.
2 Chronicles 7:13–15

<u>Read Revelation 8</u>

1. What happens in Heaven when the <u>seventh seal</u> is opened? (Read Habakkuk 2:20 and Zechariah 2:13.)

2. Why is this so unusual?

3. What does the angel in verse 3 have?

4. What does this angel do?

5. When the <u>first trumpet</u> sounded, what happened?

6. Please compare the first trumpet to the warning of Joel 2:30.

7. When the <u>second trumpet</u> sounded, what happened?

8. Please compare the second trumpet plague to Exodus 7:19–21.

9. The <u>third trumpet</u> sounded and what happened? (Read Exodus 15:23–27.)

10. The <u>fourth trumpet</u> sounded and what happened? (Read Exodus 10:21–23.)

11. Except for the grass, a third of things were struck. What do you believe is the reason for that? (Read 2 Peter 3:9.)

12. Can you find time this week to sit in silence for half an hour; focusing only on the holiness and majesty of God? Write about your experience.

13. In verse 13, what is the eagle calling out in midair and who is he calling too?

Read Revelation 9

1. In the opening of Chapter 9, what was given the key to the Abyss?

2. Do you think the "star that had fallen" could be Satan? Please read Isaiah 14:12–14 and Luke 10:18. What are your thoughts on this?

3. What came out of the Abyss when the <u>fifth trumpet</u> sounded? (Read Exodus 10:1–20.)

4. Please compare Joel 2:28–32 and Acts 2:17–21.

5. In verses 4–5, who were the locusts told to harm and for how long?

6. The four angels had been kept ready for what in verse 15?

7. The number of mounted troops, were how many?

8. What did their heads resemble?

9. What was a third of mankind killed from, when the <u>sixth trumpet</u> sounded?

10. What makes the fifth and sixth trumpets differ from the first four?

11. The power of these horses came from their _____ and _____?

12. What did "the rest of mankind" refuse to do in verses 20–21?

13. The source of an unrepentant heart is what?
    (Read Psalm 10:4, Daniel 5:20 and Obadiah 1:3.)

After discussing your answers,
Please Read Revelation 8 and 9 Aloud!

Revelation 10 and 11

Week 6

Dear Jesus, we stop for a moment to pray for the precious souls
involved in this study of your Word. Give them strength and
endurance. Help them be strong and courageous with their
testimony Lord. Make them like strong pillars in the faith.
Keep their testimony ever ready on their lips and fresh in
their heart so they can always give an answer as to why you
mean so much to them. In the sweet name of Jesus. Amen.

You've made it halfway through! Halfway through the study and
what some consider halfway through the Tribulation. We have
reached another pause in the action.

Some people think, the angel coming down from heaven in the
opening of Chapter 10 could be Jesus. This angel does have some
of the same qualities as Jesus, with a face like the sun and the
roar of a lion. Jesus is called the "Lion of the tribe of Judah" as
we learned earlier in Revelation 5:5. Scholars believe that in the
Old Testament, Jesus appeared several times as the "angel of the
LORD." Although we are not studying the angel of the LORD
here, it is interesting to note, and something for you to study in
the future if you are so inclined.

Jesus was the only one worthy to open the scroll earlier in Revelation 5. Is He the only one worthy to deliver the rest of the message? And what are the "seven thunders" speaking in Revelation 10:4? We may not know until Christ returns. One thing is for certain, we are fast approaching the end, and Jesus Christ will be revealed and acknowledged by every soul who ever lived.

> Therefore God exalted him to the highest place and gave
> him the name that is above every name, that at the name
> of Jesus every knee should bow, in heaven and on earth
> and under the earth, and every tongue acknowledge that
> Jesus Christ is Lord, to the glory of God the Father.
> Philippians 2:9–11

Before reading the chapters, let's take a look at the two witnesses of Chapter 11. There are different schools of thought on who these two are. Some people think Enoch is possibly one of these witnesses. According to Genesis 5:21–24, Enoch walked faithfully with God for 300 years, and lived for a total of 365 years. In verse 24 it says, "then he was no more, because God took him away." Hebrews 11:5–6 tells us that Enoch "did not experience death" and that "He could not be found, because God had taken him away."

Elijah is also thought to be a candidate because he did not experience death either. You will find in 2 Kings 2:11–12, Elijah being taken up to heaven in a whirlwind. Elijah also destroyed people by fire in 2 Kings 1:10–14, which is what the two witnesses do in this chapter. Another reason for considering Elijah is that he appeared along with Moses and Jesus at the Transfiguration written about in Matthew 17:1–2.

Moses is another possibility. In Deuteronomy 34, we learn that Moses was buried in Moab but "no one knows where his grave is." One of the main reasons for thinking Moses could be a witness in this pair is that Moses along with Aaron turned water to blood in Exodus 7. You will read in Revelation 11 that the two witnesses will turn waters into blood also.

A less dramatic idea is that these two witnesses will be two unknown people. Whoever they are, they are called "two olive trees" and "two lampstands." Olive oil is used to produce light for the lampstands, lampstands bear the light. These two witnesses will be producing light in an otherwise dark world. You can learn more about the making of the lampstand in Exodus 25:31–40.

Before moving on, we will look at another important issue regarding these two witnesses. Revelation 11:7 is one of my favorite scriptures. Please take note, that up to this point in their story, no one has been allowed to harm them. These two are only allowed to die when their testimony is finished. When they have finished the course set out before them by God Almighty, they are overpowered and permitted to die. For me, this brings wonderful comfort and peace. I am not leaving this world until my testimony is finished, and neither are you!

Do you have a testimony you would like to share?

Please prayerfully consider who you can share your testimony with in the days ahead. Someone somewhere needs to hear what you have been through, and he or she needs to know how God came through for you!

Read Revelation 10

Before discussing answers, if in a group,
Please invite anyone who wants to share their
testimony to do so at this time.

1. Please read Romans 1:16–32. What is God doing in these verses with people who refuse to repent?

2. Describe the angel at the opening of Chapter 10.

3. Please look up these descriptions of Jesus and compare to Revelation 10:1–4.
   Job 37:2, Hosea 11:10, Matthew 17:2, Revelation 1:14–16.

4. What did the angel have in his hand?

5. Where did the angel plant his feet, and what do you think that signifies?

6. What was John told to do in verse 4?

7. In verse 6, who does the angel swear by?

8. "There will be no more_____!"

9. Verse 7, "the mystery of _____ will be
   _____, just as he announced to his servants
   the _____."

10. The little scroll in verses 9–10 was sweet & sour. What do
    you think is the reason for this? (Read Psalm 119:103.)

Read Revelation11

1. What is John measuring in verses 1–2?

2. How long are the two witnesses prophesying?

3. What are your thoughts regarding the two witnesses being called olive trees and lampstands?

4. What happens to anyone who tries to harm the two witnesses?

5. The two witnesses were given power to do what?

6. When the two witnesses finish their testimony, what takes place?

7. Please list other names for the antichrist found in Daniel 7:8, 2 Thessalonians 2:3, 1 John 2:18 and Revelation 13:1(not the dragon).

8. What do the inhabitants of the earth do when the two witnesses are killed?

9. Which Christian holidays does this remind you of?

10. What happens in Revelation 11:11–12?

11. How many people are killed in the earthquake that follows?

12. What did the survivors in Israel do after the earthquake?

13. "The _____ _____has passed."

14. The <u>seventh trumpet</u> is now sounding. What is being heard?

15. What happens when the temple of God is opened in verse 19?

After discussing your answers,
Please Read Revelation 10 and 11 Aloud!

Revelation 12 and 13

Week 7

As we prepare to read Chapters 12 and 13, be reminded that up to this point, the antichrist has been known as a peacemaker by confirming a peace agreement with Israel for seven years. This protection will permit the nation to rebuild its temple, if not done before this time, and Israel will be reinstituting religious rituals. (Daniel 9:27 and Revelation 11:1.)

In these chapters we are still just three and a half-years into the Tribulation. You will remember from previous lessons that it is at this point the antichrist breaks the covenant with Israel. He will force the Jewish people to stop their religious ceremonies and he calls himself God in their temple. (Daniel 9:27.)

In talking with friends about end-time prophecy and the antichrist, I have learned that some people think the antichrist will come from the murdering group of people trying to rule the Middle East at this present time. I'm not sure how that could be possible, as the antichrist will initially be a peacemaker, and that particular group is certainly not into the peace process.

There is another area in the study of end-time events that people cannot seem to agree on. That is the geographic location of exactly where the antichrist comes from. Some people think, the antichrist comes from, as I said before, the Middle East. Some think he could arise from the country of Turkey or even Israel. Some people say he will arise from the Revived Roman Empire. Although we are not certain what area of the world he will come from, we can be certain he will arise.

Isaiah 14:12–15 not only describes what happens to the King of Babylon, but many scholars believe it is also describing the fall of Satan from heaven. This passage in Isaiah helps us understand that Satan thought he could be like God. Isaiah 14:14 says, "I will make myself like the Most High." In Revelation 12, we also read about the "stars" that were swept out of the sky by a "tail," the tail of the dragon, who is Satan. Scholars think these "stars" are angels that fell from heaven when Satan fell.

As you read through these chapters, pay close attention to an unholy trinity emerging. Again, there is Satan who wants to be like God. Satan will energize a human being (the antichrist/beast) who will now be a sort of counterfeit Christ. The second beast, also known as the false prophet, acts as the Holy Spirit. His mission will be to force all people to follow the first beast.

Have you ever heard someone say, the Holy Spirit is a "gentleman?" The Holy Spirit does not force anyone to accept Jesus as their own personal Savior. That is what free will is all about. Can a love be true love if forced? Our loving God wants us to freely choose Him. The ministry of our God's beautiful Holy Spirit, is to gently guide people to Jesus. The Holy Spirit opens the eyes of the lost. The Holy Spirit whispers to the hearts of the lost,

"Come, come to Jesus."

While you read these chapters, you will notice some things pointing to future events, while other things revisit the past. Here is a look at what I mean:

Events taking place in the past, Rev. 12.

V. 1–2, Israel was born as a nation. Israel and Jerusalem are spoken of several times in scripture as a woman. (Scripture references found at first question for Rev. 12.)

V. 4, Scholars believe this verse is referring to a third of the angels being cast out of heaven along with Satan, the first time. Angels are referred to as stars in Rev. 1:20. As you read the last part of verse 4, remember King Herod in Matthew 2 giving out the order to kill all male children two years old and under. This is just one example of Satan trying to remove Jesus before the set time.

V. 5, "She" (Israel) gives the world the Messiah. A male child will rule with "an iron scepter." (Also Rev. 19:15.) In verse 5 we read, "her child was snatched up to God" this is believed to be referencing the ascension of Jesus 40 days after his death. (Read Luke 24:50, Acts 1:1–11.)

Events pertaining to the middle of the Tribulation, Rev. 12.

V. 6, The woman (Israel, Jewish people) flees to a safe place where she is cared for by God. The scripture says she is there for 1260 days, which is three and a half years with each month having 30 days.

V. 7, There is a war in heaven. Satan is defeated along with his angels. They are hurled to the earth again. Cast out for the last time!

V. 14, Some people think the passage, "the wings of a great eagle" refers to America, and that America will help Israel during this time. It is possible I suppose, and that would be wonderful. However, be reminded that we have read about eagle wings earlier in this study as we read scripture from Ezekiel and Daniel. You can read more regarding eagle wings in Deuteronomy 32:10–12 and Isaiah 40:28–31.

V. 15, Water can and does symbolize several different things in scripture (another great study for you). When you read 2 Samuel 22:17–18, Psalm 18:16–17, Psalm 124 and Jeremiah 47:1–3, you will understand that in these passages "water" means enemy. The serpent "spewing" water may mean enemies are trying to invade Israel's safe place. If this is the case, we know God will rescue them. Proverbs 18:4 says "The words of the mouth are deep waters, but the fountain of wisdom is a rushing stream." Could this water possibly be a wave of anti-Semitic speech and hatred toward "the woman?"

V. 16, The earth opening its mouth might mean an earthquake will swallow the invaders.

Events in the future, revisiting the past, Rev. 13.

V. 2 The beast John sees has some of the same qualities as the beasts in Daniel 7. The leopard, the bear and the lion are all kingdoms from ancient history. The 4th kingdom in Daniel 7 is the kingdom of the antichrist, and is still in the future.

On his television program, *Christ in Prophecy*, I have heard Dr. David Reagan say, "If the plain sense makes sense, don't look for any other sense or you will end up with nonsense."

I really like that statement. It "makes sense." And when in doubt, let the Bible interpret itself. Look for scripture to support everything you are studying. Rely on the Holy Spirit of God to open your eyes for understanding. It is far too dangerous to misinterpret the Word of God. Always remain teachable and open to change if what you think to be right, does not agree with scripture.

Remember to keep Jesus at the center. The
Holy Spirit will show you the way!

Read Revelation 12

1. The woman in verse 1 is representative of who or what? (Read Genesis 37:9, Isaiah 49:14–26, 54:1–7 and 66:7–9 also Micah 4:10 and 5:2–3.)

2. Who is the child? (Luke 1:26–38.)

3. What is interesting about the number of stars in her crown? (Revelation 7:5–8.)

4. The red dragon had _____ heads, 10_____ and _____ crowns.

5. The tail of the red dragon did what?

6. Where did the "woman" go and why?

7. How long was the "woman" taken care of?

8. War broke out where and between whom?

9. What happened to the great dragon?

10. Who is the dragon? (Revelation 12:9.)

11. List the names for Satan given in verses 9–10.

12. Who does verse 10 mean "the accuser of our brothers and sisters" is?

13. What does Romans 8:1–2 say?

14. What does Revelation 12:11 mean to you?

15. What did the dragon do when he saw he had been hurled to the earth, verse 13?

16. When you hear news about Israel, do you notice anti-Semitism?

17. What did the LORD say to Abram in Genesis 12:1–3?

18. Who else is Satan waging war against?

Read Revelation 13

1. The beast has _____horns, _____heads and 10 _____.

2. Please read Revelation 17:9–10. The _____ heads are _____

   And also, _____.

3. What was written on each head, Revelation 13:1?

4. Please read Daniel 7:24 and Revelation 17:12. What do the horns represent?

5. Please compare the animals of Daniel 7:3–8 to the animals of Revelation 13:2–4.

6. Please read Daniel 7:19–25. Describe the 4th kingdom.

7. In Revelation 13:4, who did the people worship and why?

8. In Revelation 13:5–8, please describe what the beast has been given.

9. Read Daniel 11:36. What does this king do?

10. Does Revelation 13:10 read like it's happening in the world today?

11. What does this call for?

12. In Revelation 13:11–12, there is a second beast introduced. Describe this beast.

13. This second beast is known as the false prophet.

    What is the false prophet doing in Revelation 13:13?

14. What does the false prophet force all people to do?

15. What does this call for?

After discussing answers,
Please Read Revelation 12 and 13 Aloud!

Revelation 14 and 15

Week 8

In Chapter 12 we read about a battle over the baby. In Chapter 13, we read about the wickedness of Satan. We read about the first beast, which is the antichrist, and the second beast, who is the false prophet. In Chapter 14, we have reached another brief interruption in the action. You will remember this is known as a parenthetical pause.

The 144,000 male virgin Jews are offered as firstfruits. This means they are the very finest. God had much to say about firstfruits in the Old Testament. It is interesting to read about.

If you would like to read more about firstfruits, see Exodus 34:26, Leviticus 23:9–14, and Deuteronomy 26:1–11. For more reading on the feasts and festivals of the Lord, read all of Leviticus 23.

The Feasts of the Lord is a wonderful teaching written by Mark Biltz. I highly recommend it, as it is filled with a wealth of information. According to Pastor Biltz, three feasts have not yet been fulfilled. These feasts (festivals, appointed times) are Yom Teruah, Yom Kippur and Sukkot. Each of these feasts are observed at harvest time in the fall. The month of Tishrei is the holiest time of the year for the Jewish people. Tishrei takes place during the months of September and October on the Gregorian calendar.

Yom Teruah, is also known as Rosh Hashanah, The Feast of Trumpets and The Day of the Trumpet Blast. Yom Teruah is the feast that no one knew the day or the hour it would begin (Sound familiar? See Matthew 24:36) because it coincides with the cycle of the moon. Rosh Hashanah means "head of the year." On this day, the creation of Adam and Eve is commemorated as well as the binding of Isaac by his father, Abraham. (Genesis 22:1–19.) During this feast there are one hundred blasts from a trumpet or shofar. (1 Corinthians 15:52.) Many people believe that it will be during this feast that the "catching away" or "rapture" will happen.

Yom Kippur is also known as The Day of Atonement and The Fast. This feast is considered the most holy day of the year for the Jewish people. It is a time of prayer, reflection and fasting. This highest of holy days is a time of forgiving others, yourself and for being reconciled to God. This is a day of rest and a day of denying oneself. Many believe that this feast will coincide with Christ's second coming and thus be fulfilled at that time. When Christ comes for a second time, plants his feet on the Mount of Olives, it will be a day of reckoning to be sure. A Day of Atonement. (Zechariah 14:4.)

The third feast is Sukkot. Also known as The Feast of Tabernacles, The Feast of Booths (Tents), The Feast of The Ingathering and The Feast of Nations. This is a seven-day celebration with a closing ceremony on the eighth day. Sukkot is a time to celebrate the fall harvest and it is to be symbolic of the forty years that the Israelites spent in the wilderness living in temporary shelters. This feast will be celebrated through the thousand-year reign of Christ. (Zechariah 14:16–19.)

As you know, harvest time is a time to reap what you sow. Winning souls for the Kingdom of God is pictured as a harvest in John 4:34–38. Harvesting is also used as a picture of God's judgment in Joel 3:13 and Matthew 13:24–30, along with verses 36–43. While you study the harvest of Revelation 14:14–20 this week, know that some bible scholars believe these passages refer to the battle of Armageddon, while others believe this is the rapture of the church. The battle of Armageddon is actually not happening at this point in our study, but many scholars believe it is being referenced in Revelation 14:14–20. Just like in Chapters 12 and 13, some things pointed to the future, and some things pointed back in time. You will see this happening again in Chapter 14. One scene that is pointing ahead is this battle which will take place in Revelation 19 but as I said, is referenced in Revelation 14:14–20. You can also see this same battle being referenced in Joel 3:9–15.

In Chapter 14, we read about an angel that is gathering grapes from the earth's vine. In the Book of John, Chapter 15, Jesus says, "I am the vine." If you read Psalm 80, Isaiah 5 and Matthew 21, you will see that the nation of Israel is also considered a vine. In today's lesson, we learn that the earth's vine is ripe for judgment. Remember now, we as Christians are not appointed to wrath, as we saw in the beginning of this study. As you will see while reading verse 19, the grapes are being thrown into the "winepress of God's wrath." Therefore, I do not believe that Rev. 14:14–20 is referencing the rapture of the church.

I would like to draw your attention to what our awesome God is doing in Revelation 14:6. He is sending an angel to preach the gospel! Amazing! Our God scolds and He also saves. He disciplines and He rescues. Although our God is merciful, gracious and kind, we will see during our study this week that his beautiful tender mercy does have an ending.

Revelation 14:8 speaks of Babylon the Great. Babylon is God's name for the world's system that the beast(antichrist) will be the head of. The particular location of the actual antichrist's headquarters is still a mystery. However, some say it is ancient Babylon rebuilt, which Iraq was working on before the Gulf War took place in the early nineteen nineties. Some say that Babylon is the United States of America; however, John does call it a city several times. Some think it could possibly be New York City, while others say it might be a village in New York State, which is actually named Babylon. Many scholars believe Babylon is Rome. In any case, if the most brilliant scholars and theologians aren't sure, then let's consider simply what scripture says. "The name written on her forehead was a mystery." Revelation 17:5.

In Revelation 15 we meet the seven angels with the seven last plagues. In Revelation 5 we read about golden bowls filled with the prayers of God's people. The bowls in Revelation 15 are filled with plagues. When these bowls are poured out, the wrath of the living God is completed. As Chapter 15 opens, everything seems quite calm. It begins peaceful. There is a sea of glass. People are singing and making melody to God.

Then you read that angels are preparing for the last act of retribution ordered by a holy God. We have come so far into the Tribulation and there are still people who refuse to repent. The pride of one's heart is a puzzle. Please continue to pray for the lost.

<u>Read Revelation 14</u>

1. Who is the Lamb in verse 1? (John 1:29, 36.)

2. What do we know about the 144,000 from verses 1–5 and previous lessons?

3. What did the 144,000 have written on their foreheads?

4. Who were the only ones able to learn the song of verse 3?

5. What was the angel in verse 6 proclaiming?

6. The angel in verse 8 is saying what?

7. What is the angel in verse 9–11 saying?

8. This calls for what?

9. How does verse 13 encourage you?

10. What is happening in verse 14?

11. From the following scriptures, who do we learn is "one like the son of man?"
    Daniel 7:13–14, Matthew 16:13–17, 20:28, Mark 8:31, 38 and Revelation 1:13.

12. What are your thoughts regarding Revelation 14:15–20?

<u>Read Revelation 15</u>

1. How many angels are there and how many plagues did they have?

2. What is completed with these plagues?

3. What did the sea look like, and who was standing beside it?

4. What were they holding, and what were they doing?

5. Who gave them what they were holding?

6. What song did they sing?

7. Write some of your favorite lines from the songs of Moses. (Exodus 15:1–18 and Deuteronomy 32:1–43.)

8. Read Deuteronomy 31:14–19. Who told Moses to write the song of Deuteronomy 32?

9. The "covenant law" is what? (Exodus 32:15–16 and Exodus 34:27–28.)

10. Please read Exodus 40:34–35 and 2 Chronicles 7:1–3. Write down what filled the tabernacle and temple.

11. What was the temple filled with in Isaiah 6:1–4 and Revelation 15:8?

12. What were the bowls filled with in Revelation 15?

After discussing the answers,
Please Read Revelation 14 and 15 Aloud!

Revelation 16 and 17

Week 9

With Chapter 16, we move ever and ever closer to the end of life on planet Earth, as people have known it up to now. We will read in the chapters ahead God's mercy will end, and his wrath will be completed (Rev. 15:1). The last of the seven judgments have arrived, and so has the destruction of Babylon (the world's economic & political system, Rev. 18) along with the judgment of the religious system of the day, spoken of as the "prostitute" in Revelation 17. Obviously, the opposite of a prostitute is a pure bride. The "pure bride" spoken of in scripture is the Christ following church. This church is who Christ is returning for. This false religion has long been evident on the earth, but today we see long-held biblical beliefs being shattered by newly-created laws. We are also seeing the worship of Satan dominate headlines. If you watch the news, you see evil being accepted as good.

> Woe to those who call evil good and good evil,
> who put darkness for light and light for darkness,
> who put bitter for sweet and sweet for bitter.
> Isaiah 5:20

Nation after nation is exchanging good for evil and evil for good. People who honor God and his word are made to seem hateful,

nding in the way of progress. In Matthew 22:36–39
.ed,

> Teacher, which is the greatest commandment in the Law?
> Jesus replied: Love the Lord your God with all your heart
> and with all your soul and with all your mind. This is the
> first and greatest commandment. And the second is like it:
> Love your neighbor as yourself.

The very simple truth is, we love. However, we do not accept sin in any way, shape or form. We cannot be compromising Christians. We love and then we pray. We need only to rely on God's Spirit to change lives and hearts. It is beyond our capability to change people.

> He is wooing you from the jaws of distress
> to a spacious place free from restriction,
> to the comfort of your table laden with choice food.
> Job 36:16

Remember a few pages back, you read that the Holy Spirit of God gently guides people to Jesus? This is one verse that shows us that.

The word "woo" means to make an effort, and try to gain the love of someone. The Holy Spirit has been wooing you your whole life. It is the Holy Spirit who pulls at your heart and draws you to a relationship with Christ. Not only does the Spirit of God woo individuals, he has also been known to woo nations.

> Therefore I am now going to allure her; I will lead
> her into the wilderness and speak tenderly to her.
>
> Hosea 2:14

Although Hosea speaks of his relationship with his wife here, these passages also represent Israel's relationship with God. Hosea's wife was unfaithful and Israel has been unfaithful to God, by repeatedly falling into idol worship.

The love of God is steadfast and unchanging. It truly is a love affair gone wild. The love we can experience from God is a love that offers an unlimited amount of chances to begin anew. Because the heart of God longs for people and nations to repent and turn to him.

Read Revelation 16

1. Where was the voice coming from, and what was being said in verse 1?

2. When the first bowl was poured out what happened?

3. Please read Exodus 9:8–11 and Deuteronomy 28:27, 35. Then write down how the sores in Revelation 16:2 differ or are the same.

4. When the second bowl was poured out what happened?

5. How many living things in the sea die?

6. The third bowl was poured out and what happened?

7. Please read Exodus 7:14–25. Are these plagues similar to the second and third bowl judgments?

8. In your own words, what did the angel in charge of the waters say in Revelation 16:5–6?

9. What responded and what was said in verse 7?

10. The <u>fourth bowl</u> was poured out. Explain what happened. (Read Malachi 4:1.)

11. Who is in control of these plagues? (Revelation16: 9.)

12. What did the people refuse to do?

13. What happened when the <u>fifth bowl</u> was poured out? (Read Exodus 10:21–23.)

14. Whose kingdom was plunged into darkness?

15. What did people do when the fifth bowl was poured out?

16. What did they refuse to do?

17. The sixth angel poured out the <u>sixth bowl</u> and what happened?

18. What did this prepare the way for?

19. Where do the impure spirits come from and what do they do? (Verses 13, 14 and 16.)

20. Who is speaking in verse 15?

21. The <u>seventh bowl</u> is poured out. Describe what is happening.

22. How much did the hailstones weigh?

23. People did what when the hailstones fell on them?

24. What happened in Exodus 9:22–26?

Read Revelation 17

1. What does the angel in verse 1 invite John to do?

2. Do you have an opinion as to whom or what you think the prostitute is?

3. The opposite of a prostitute is what?

4. After John was carried away in the Spirit, what did John see?

5. The woman in verse 3 is identified as what in Revelation 17:18?

6. Take time to read Jeremiah 51 regarding ancient Babylon. You have already read Revelation 17, now glance through Revelation 18. These chapters in Revelation are speaking of a

future Babylon. Please list some similarities regarding ancient and future Babylon. (Ex. Rev. 17:1 says "who sits by many waters" Jer. 51:13 says "who live by many waters.")

7. What was written on the woman's head?

8. The woman was drunk with what?

9. You have answered this question once before, in Chapter 13. As a refresher; what are the seven heads and ten horns? (Revelation 17:9–10, 12 and Daniel 7:24.)

10. The beast that John saw in verse 8, comes up from where? (Revelation 11:7.)

11. "The inhabitants of the earth, whose names have not been written in the book of life, from the creation of the world will be _____when they see the beast."

12. **Why** were the inhabitants of the earth _____?

13. "The beast, which you saw once was, now is _____, and yet will _____."

14. People have different thoughts on Revelation17:8.
    Some think this may be the Roman Empire rising up again, while others think Hitler or Stalin or even Nimrod could rise from the dead. What are your thoughts on this passage?

15. This calls for what?

16. Five kings have _____, one is, the other has _____.

17. The "eighth king belongs to the seven." Write down what you think this could mean.

18. Is it possible the eighth king, the beast and the antichrist are the same?

19. What have the ten horns not received yet?

20. How long will the ten horns have authority?

21. These ten have _____ purpose and what do they do?

22. "but the Lamb will _____"

23. Who is the Lamb in verse 14?

24. Who is with him when he triumphs?

25. What do the waters represent in verse 15?

26. The beast and the ten horns do what to the prostitute?

27. What has God done in verse 17?

After discussing answers,
Please Read Revelation 16 and 17 Aloud!

Revelation 18 and 19

Week 10

Last week we glanced at Revelation 18. This week we take a more in-depth look, and learn more about Babylon. Ancient Babylon was called, "the jewel of the kingdoms" in Isaiah 13:19.

As we read further, God issues a strong word to this kingdom through the Prophet Isaiah.

> Babylon, the jewel of the kingdoms, the pride and glory of the Babylonians, will be overthrown by God like Sodom and Gomorrah. She will never be inhabited or lived in through all generations; there no nomads will pitch their tents, there no shepherds will rest their flocks. But desert creatures will lie there, jackals will fill her houses; there the owls will dwell, and there the wild goats will leap about. Hyenas will inhabit her strongholds, jackals her luxurious palaces. Her time is at hand and her days will not be prolonged.
> Isaiah 13:19-22

The Babylon here in Chapter 18 does not sound much different than the one back in ancient times. We read in this chapter, whether the world's economic and political system, or an actual modern-day city, or both, Babylon is luxurious and quite wealthy. It has made nations and their kings rich. It is also corrupted by sin and wickedness. It has become a "haunt for every impure spirit."

Babylon the Great has now fallen, and with the fall comes one more plea from Heaven. "Come out of her, my people," (Revelation 18:4). As people who follow Jesus Christ, we must always be ready to separate ourselves from this world, and never be complicit in sin. God however is quick to forgive us when we do make mistakes and repent.

> as far as the east is from the west, so far has he
> removed our transgressions from us.
> Psalm 103:12

It seems everyone is mourning over this evil Babylon, except the people of God. The people of God are rejoicing! Chapter 19 is the chapter where Jesus Christ returns to earth. This is his 2nd coming.

> On that day his feet will stand on the Mount of Olives,
> east of Jerusalem, and the Mount of Olives will be split in
> two from east to west, forming a great valley, with half of
> the mountain moving north and half moving south."
> Zechariah 14:4

<u>Read Revelation 18</u>

1. The angel in verse 1 has what?

2. What happened to the earth when the angel appeared?

3. Babylon the Great has become what?

4. What do you think this means?

5. How many nations have drunk the maddening wine of her adulteries?

6. "The merchants of the earth grew _____ from her _____ _____."

7. Share your thoughts on verses 4–8.

8. What did the kings of the earth do in verses 9–10?

9. How long did it take for Babylon's doom to come?

10. The merchants of the earth do what in verses 11–17?

11. Every sea captain does what in verses 17–19?

12. Who is told to rejoice in verse 20?

13. What did the mighty angel throw into the sea?

14. What happens to Babylon in verses 21–23?

15. What was found in Babylon?

Read Revelation 19

1. What was the great multitude shouting?

2. What did it sound like?

3. What did the twenty-four elders and four living creatures do?

4. Where is God?

5. What did the great multitude sound like in verse 6?

6. What is your favorite part of verses 6–8?

7. Who are the "Blessed" ones in verse 9? (Read Matthew 8:11 and Luke 14:15.)

8. "These are the_____words of God."

9. Who is invited to the wedding supper of the Lamb? (John 3:3 and 1 John 5:12–13.)

10. What are the "fellow servant" & "your brothers and sisters" holding onto in verse 10?

11. What is the definition of prophecy?

12. Describe the rider on this white horse.

13. Verse 13 says his name is what? (Read John 1:1, John 1:14 and Hebrews 4:12.)

14. Who is following him on white horses, dressed in linen?

15. What is coming out of his mouth?

16. In the last part of verse 15, "He treads the _____ with the fury of his wrath." (Read Isaiah 63:1-6.)

17. What is written on his robe and his thigh?

18. What are the birds told to do in verse 17?

19. The beast (antichrist), the kings of the earth and armies did what in verse 19?

    (We have now arrived at the battle of Armageddon, spoken of in Rev. 14:14–20 and Rev. 16:14, 16.)

20. What happened to the beast and false prophet in verse 20?

21. What happened to the rest of the army?

After discussing answers,
Please Read Revelation 18 and 19 Aloud!

Revelation 20 and 21

Week 11

We are now entering the thousand-year reign of Christ, also known as the Millennium or the Messianic Kingdom, where the "wolf will live with the lamb." (Isaiah 11:6.)

During this thousand-year period, Jesus Christ will reign as King, and there is peace on the earth.

Scholars believe Isaiah 11:6−9 and Isaiah 65:20−25 speak of this peaceful kingdom. It seems as though there will be children born during this period, according to these scriptures, and these children will need to make a decision as to whether or not they will follow Jesus. In the scripture mentioned, infants will live more than a few days and anyone who dies before one hundred years of age, will be thought of as a child, and cursed.

A beautiful and peaceful society does not and cannot change a person's heart. So the hearts of these people will be tested. This is the reason for Satan to be released for a short time at the end of the thousand-year period. At the end of the Millennium, there is one final battle between good and evil, found in Revelation 20.

In Revelation 20 verse 8 we see the titles of Gog and Magog. These are thought to be symbolic for the nations of the world, not the Gog and Magog spoken of in Ezekiel 38 and 39. The nations of Revelation 20:8 come from the four corners of the earth, when Satan goes out to deceive them. The war spoken of in Ezekiel 38 and 39 are several nations "called to arms" by the Sovereign Lord himself. He says to the "chief prince" Gog, from the land of Magog, "I am against you Gog."(Ezekiel 38:3 and Ezekiel 39:1.)

In Revelation 20 the target is Jerusalem, and this war comes to nothing, because the Lord intervenes. The Ezekiel war takes place against Israel. Many scholars believe the war in Ezekiel 38 and 39 takes place just before the Tribulation, or soon after the Tribulation begins. They believe "Gog" to be a Russian leader obviously coming from Russia ("Magog"). Some scholars believe however, "Gog" is the leader of Turkey, with "Magog" being Turkey. The area that once was the land of Magog sits close to the Turkish and Russian borders. This could explain why opinions differ on whom Gog and Magog actually are. Whomever it is and wherever they come from, there is war coming. Praise God, He is the Victor!

Read Revelation 20

    1. Where is the angel coming from?

    2. What does the angel have, and what is he holding?

    3. What does the angel do in verses 2–3?

    4. Satan will be set free for a short time. When?

    5. The souls of who were seen in verse 4?

    6. What else does verse 4 say about these souls?

7. What does Satan do in verses 7–8?

8. What happens to those who come against God's people?

9. What happens to the devil and the false prophet?

10. In verses 11–15, what is happening at the great white throne?

11. Who is thrown into the lake of fire?

12. What is the second death?

<u>Read Revelation 21</u>

1. John saw a new what?

2. What happened to the first earth and the first heaven?

3. There was no longer any what?

4. Where did the new city come from and what was its name?

5. The voice coming from the throne said what in verses 3–4?

6. Write down one thing that stands out to you in verses 5–8.

7. Who carried John away in the Spirit?

8. How many gates and how many angels does John see?

9. What is written on the gates and where were they located?

10. The wall of the city had how many foundations and what was written on them?

11. The measurements of the city were_____ high, _____long & _____wide.

12. How thick was the wall, and what was it made of?

13. What is the city made of?

14. The gates were made from what?

15. What was the great street made of?

16. The city does not need the _____ or the _____.

17. Who gives the city its light, and who is its lamp?

18. When do the gates shut?

19. What will never enter the city?

20. Who will enter?

After discussing your answers,
Please Read Revelation 20 and 21 Aloud!

Revelation 22

Week12

We are here! We have arrived!
You have waited your whole life for this day.
Your loved ones are here.
No doubt by now you've probably already
hugged and kissed many of them.
Some of them may have died in their
youth and you questioned God;
it crushed you.
Some may have passed away in old age,
the pain not lessened by that.
It remained like a fresh wound as though it happened yesterday.
But not today.
Today,
at this moment, instantly your grief is gone.
As fast as a blink, your heart felt whole.
The tears that forever stained your cheeks are now forever gone.
Oh there are no tears here, only love and life eternal.
Our King is here too; He sits on his throne.
He has waited a lifetime for us to come home.
We bow; we sing; we praise his name.
All Glory, All Honor
To our God, He reigns!

Read Revelation 22

1. Where does the water of life flow from?

2. What is on each side of the river, and what do they do?

3. What is used to heal the nations?

4. The throne of God and the Lamb are where?

5. What do the Lord's servants do?

6. "They will see_____ _____ and _____
    _____will be on their foreheads."

7. There will be no more_____.

8. In verse 6, the angel says, "These words are _____ and _____."

9. What does Jesus say in verse 7?

10. Who is "Blessed" in verse 7?

11. In verse 10, the angel says, "Do not seal up" what?

12. Why are they not sealed up?

13. What are your thoughts on verse 11?

14. Verse 12, "Look, I am _____!

15. What is he bringing with him?

16. "Blessed are those who _____their robes."

17. Who may go through the gates?

18. Who is outside the city?

19. Who is the testimony for in verse 16?

20. Jesus says in verse 16, "I am the _____ and the _____ of David and the bright _____ _____."

21. What do the Spirit and the Bride say?

22. What are the warnings in verses 18 and 19?

23. What will happen if words are added or taken away?

24. What are the last words of Jesus in Revelation 22:20?

25. Are you ready to meet the Savior of your soul?

Almighty God is the lover of each soul. Throughout the Book of Revelation, God is warning and wooing people. Warning that danger, judgment and eternal damnation are ahead, while also still inviting people to repent. The Book of Revelation is God informing us of what is going to happen.

Revelation 1:1 says:

> The revelation from Jesus Christ, which God gave him to show his servants what must soon take place.

Although he was king, Jesus humbled himself and laid his life down for each one of us. There is no greater love. And there is no other way to escape judgment and experience eternal life other than believing in Jesus Christ and accepting him as Savior. Scripture says:

> Salvation is found in no one else, for there
> is no other name under heaven given to
> mankind by which we must be saved.
> Acts 4:12

Come, come to Jesus.

After discussing answers,
Please Read Revelation 22 Aloud!

THAT HEAVENLY PLACE

Julie Peddie Fitchuk
Revelation 19, 20, 21, 22
Copyright Sept 28, 2015

(Verse 1)
One day as I enter that Heavenly Place
The gates are opened wide, my loved ones are inside
So nice to see them after all this time

As I look around, my eyes cannot believe
The beauty, the splendor of this place I can't conceive
All of my life I've waited for this day
The books will be opened oh and I'm gonna stay

Chorus
And there are no tears here, all sorrow has disappeared
There is no more sun, there is no more night
The Morning Star shines bright, His face is the light

(Verse 2)
There's a home you built for me, it's that mansion on that hill
The street is made of gold just like the stories we've been told
There are trees that line the street, their leaves heal the world
And there's a river, crystal clear, flowing from Your throne

(Verse 3)
Again and again the voices rang out singing praise
The choir filled with millions and millions and millions

And they sang Hallelujah, Praise the Lord, Praise to our God

There is none like you, You make all things new

The King of Kings and Lord of Lords, You are faithful and You are true

(Tag)

One day will you enter that Heavenly Place

The gates are open wide, are your loved ones inside

And the books will be opened are you gonna stay

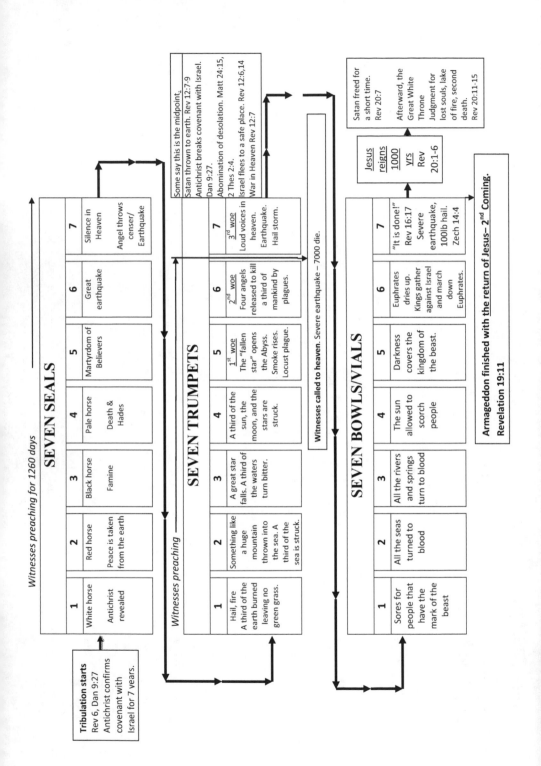

SEVEN SEALS

Witnesses preaching for 1260 days

Tribulation starts
Rev 6, Dan 9:27 Antichrist confirms covenant with Israel for 7 years.

1	2	3	4	5	6	7
White horse	Red horse	Black horse	Pale horse	Martyrdom of Believers	Great earthquake	Silence in Heaven
Antichrist revealed	Peace is taken from the earth	Famine	Death & Hades			Angel throws censer/ Earthquake

Some say this is the midpoint.
Satan thrown to earth. Rev 12:7-9
Antichrist breaks covenant with Israel. Dan 9:27.
Abomination of desolation. Matt 24:15, 2 Thes 2:4.
Israel flees to a safe place. Rev 12:6,14
War in Heaven Rev 12:7

SEVEN TRUMPETS

Witnesses preaching

1	2	3	4	5	6	7
Hail, fire A third of the earth burned leaving no green grass.	Something like a huge mountain thrown into the sea. A third of the sea is struck.	A great star falls. A third of the waters turn bitter.	A third of the sun, the moon, and the stars are struck.	1st woe The "fallen star" opens the Abyss. Smoke rises. Locust plague.	2nd woe Four angels released to kill a third of mankind by plagues.	3rd woe Loud voices in heaven. Earthquake. Hail storm.

Witnesses called to heaven. Severe earthquake – 7000 die.

SEVEN BOWLS/VIALS

1	2	3	4	5	6	7
Sores for people that have the mark of the beast	All the seas turned to blood	All the rivers and springs turn to blood	The sun allowed to scorch people	Darkness covers the kingdom of the beast.	Euphrates dries up. Kings gather against Israel and march down Euphrates.	"It is done!" Rev 16:17 Severe earthquake, 100lb hail. Zech 14:4

Armageddon finished with the return of Jesus– 2nd Coming.
Revelation 19:11

Jesus reigns 1000 yrs Rev 20:1-6

Satan freed for a short time. Rev 20:7

Afterward, the Great White Throne Judgment for lost souls, lake of fire, second death. Rev 20:11-15

114